How to Create and Sell Online Courses That Actually Make Money

A Step-by-Step Guide to Creating and Selling Profitable Online Courses with SEO Strategies to Get More Students

The Fix-It Guy

Table of Contents

Introduction

Hey there, aspiring course creators, digital entrepreneurs, and knowledge enthusiasts! Are you tired of sifting through a sea of online course advice, hoping to find that golden nugget of wisdom that will turn your passion into profit? Do you dream of creating online courses that not only educate but also generate a steady stream of income? Well, guess what? You've just stumbled upon the ultimate roadmap to transforming your knowledge into cold, hard cash, "How to Create and Sell Online Courses That Make Money: A Step-by-Step Guide to Creating and Selling Profitable Online Courses with SEO Strategies to Get More Students."

Picture this: a life where you wake up every morning, excited to check your email, not because you're expecting a message from your boss, but because you're anticipating notifications of new course enrollments and the sweet sound of cha-ching in your virtual cash register. Imagine having the freedom to share your expertise with the world, making a difference in people's lives, all while raking in the dough. Sounds like a dream, right? Well, buckle up, because we're about to turn that dream into your reality!

In the pages of this book, I won't just throw generic advice at you and leave you to figure it out on your own.

No way! We're going to embark on a thrilling journey together, where I'll guide you through the exhilarating highs and inevitable lows of creating, marketing and profiting from online courses. Whether you're a seasoned educator, a budding entrepreneur, or someone with a passion itching to be shared, this book is your ticket to the lucrative world of online education.

We'll dive deep into the nitty-gritty details, uncovering secrets that successful course creators have guarded like precious treasures. You'll learn how to identify your unique niche, craft compelling course content, optimize your courses for search engines, and launch with a bang that reverberates across the digital landscape. Get ready to master the art of engaging your audience, handling student inquiries like a pro, and analyzing your course performance to keep improving.

But hold on, it's not all serious business here! Prepare for a sprinkle of humor, a dash of inspiration, and a heap of practical, actionable advice that you can implement right away. I promise we'll make this journey not just informative, but downright fun. So, grab your favorite beverage, find a comfy spot, and let's embark on this adventure together. By the time you reach the last page, you won't just be equipped with knowledge; you'll be armed with the confidence to turn your passion into a thriving online course empire.

Chapter 1

Why Online Courses Matter

The Rise of E-Learning

In this chapter, we delve into the fundamental reasons why online courses matter in today's digital landscape. We explore the rise of e-learning and the advantages of selling online courses, shedding light on the transformative power of this educational revolution.

The twenty-first century has witnessed a dramatic shift in the way we learn and share knowledge. E-learning, or electronic learning, has emerged as a game-changer in the education industry, disrupting traditional classroom models and opening up new possibilities for both educators and learners.

Access to Learning Anytime, Anywhere: One of the most remarkable aspects of e-learning is its accessibility. It allows people to acquire knowledge from the comfort of their homes, cafes, libraries, or anywhere with an internet connection. This flexibility means that you can learn at your own pace, fitting education into your busy schedule.

A World of Topics at Your Fingertips: Online courses cover an astonishing array of subjects, from coding and cooking to astrophysics and zoology. You're not limited by geographical boundaries or the availability of local courses. Whatever you're passionate about or interested in, there's likely an online course waiting for you.

Learn from the Best: E-learning offers access to world-renowned experts and educators. You can enroll in courses taught by experts in their fields, individuals you might never have the opportunity to learn from in a traditional setting. The digital realm breaks down geographical barriers, making knowledge more accessible than ever.

Cost-Efficiency: Traditional education can be expensive, with tuition fees, textbooks, and commuting costs adding up. Online courses are often more affordable, and many are even offered for free. You can save money while still gaining valuable knowledge.

Personalized Learning: E-learning platforms often use advanced algorithms to tailor the learning experience to each student. This means you receive customized recommendations and resources, helping you learn more effectively.

Interactive and Engaging: E-learning isn't just about reading text on a screen. Modern online courses use a variety of multimedia elements, quizzes, assignments, and discussion forums to make learning engaging and interactive.

Advantages of Selling Online Courses

Passive Income Potential: Selling online courses can generate passive income streams. Once your course is created and published, it can continue to earn money for you, even while you sleep.

Global Reach: When you sell courses online, your potential audience is not limited to your local community or country. You can attract students from all over the world, expanding your reach and impact.

Low Overhead Costs: Unlike traditional brick-and-mortar education, creating and selling online courses doesn't require a physical classroom or costly infrastructure. Your main investment is your time and expertise.

Creative Expression: Online courses offer a creative outlet for sharing your knowledge and passion. You can design your courses in a way that reflects your unique teaching style and expertise.

Elevated Brand and Authority: Being a successful online course creator can elevate your personal or professional brand. It establishes you as an expert in your field, opening doors to new opportunities and partnerships.

Chapter 2

Identifying Your Niche

Choosing the Right Course Topic

In this pivotal chapter, we'll embark on the journey of finding your unique niche in the vast landscape of online education. Crafting a successful online course starts with honing in on a topic that not only excites you but also resonates with your target audience. Let's dive into the essential steps of choosing the right course topic and researching market demand to ensure your online venture is both fulfilling and financially rewarding.

1. Choosing the Right Course Topic

Follow Your Passion: What are you deeply passionate about? What knowledge or skills do you possess that make you light up when talking about them? Your passion will infuse your course with energy and authenticity, making it more engaging for your students.

Assess Your Expertise: Reflect on your expertise and experiences. What are you exceptionally good at? Your expertise forms the foundation of your course. Teaching something you know inside-out not only boosts your confidence but also instills trust in your students.

Identify Pain Points: Consider the common challenges faced by people in your field of interest. What problems can you solve for them? Courses that address specific pain points or provide practical solutions tend to attract eager learners.

Evaluate Market Trends: Stay updated with current trends and developments in your field. Emerging trends can signify growing interest and demand, making them excellent topics for your course. However, balance trendiness with timeless knowledge to ensure your course remains relevant in the long run.

Researching Market Demand

Keyword Research: Use tools like Google Keyword Planner to identify popular search terms related to your niche. High search volumes indicate a strong interest in specific topics. Additionally, explore long-tail keywords, as they often represent more targeted and eager audiences.

Competitor Analysis: Investigate existing courses and educational platforms within your niche. Analyze their content, pricing, and student reviews. Identify gaps in their offerings or areas where you can provide a unique perspective. Your goal is to offer something distinctive and valuable.

Surveys and Feedback: Reach out to your target audience through surveys or social media platforms. Ask questions about their learning needs, preferences, and challenges. Direct feedback from potential students can provide invaluable insights into the demand for specific topics and the features learners seek in a course.

Online Communities: Participate in forums, social media groups, or online communities related to your niche. Engage in discussions and observe the questions people frequently ask. Understanding the concerns and interests of your target audience directly from their conversations can guide your course topic selection.

By the end of this chapter, you'll have a crystal-clear understanding of your niche, armed with insights into what your audience is searching for and how you can fulfill those needs.

Chapter 3

Planning Your Course

Defining Learning Objectives

Welcome to the blueprint phase of your online course creation journey. In this chapter, we'll explore the crucial steps of planning your course, ensuring that your educational masterpiece is not only well-organized but also profoundly impactful. By defining clear learning objectives and structuring your course content effectively, you'll create a learning experience that engages, informs, and empowers your students.

1. Defining Learning Objectives

Clarity is Key: Start by defining clear, specific, and achievable learning objectives for your course. What do you want your students to know, understand, or be able to do by the end of the course? Well-defined objectives provide a roadmap for your course content and guide your students toward their goals.

Consider Bloom's Taxonomy: Bloom's Taxonomy categorizes learning objectives into different levels, ranging from basic knowledge recall to advanced skills like analysis and creation. Tailor your objectives to different levels of Bloom's Taxonomy, ensuring a well-rounded learning experience that challenges and nurtures your students.

Measurable Outcomes: Ensure your objectives are measurable. Use action verbs like "analyze," "create," or "evaluate" to describe what students will accomplish. Measurable outcomes not only help students track their progress but also allow you to assess the effectiveness of your teaching methods.

Structuring Your Course Content

Module Breakdown: Divide your course into logical modules or sections. Each module should focus on a specific topic or skill set. Structuring your content this way makes it easier for students to digest information and progress through the course systematically.

Introduction and Orientation: Start your course with a compelling introduction that outlines the course objectives, what students can expect to learn, and the benefits of completing the course. An orientation module that familiarizes students with the course platform, resources, and communication channels enhances the overall learning experience.

Engaging Multimedia: Integrate a variety of multimedia elements such as videos, interactive quizzes, podcasts, and visual aids. Different learning styles benefit from diverse content formats, keeping the course engaging and stimulating for all participants.

Clear Progression: Create a clear learning path for your students. Guide them through the course in a logical sequence, ensuring that each module builds upon the previous one. Clearly outline prerequisites for advanced topics, if applicable, to maintain a smooth learning flow.

Practical Application: Incorporate real-life examples, case studies, and practical exercises. Encourage students to apply the knowledge they've gained. Practical application not only reinforces learning but also boosts confidence and retention.

Assessment and Feedback: Include quizzes, assignments, and assessments to evaluate students' understanding. Constructive feedback is invaluable; it highlights strengths, addresses weaknesses, and motivates students to improve. Use assessments strategically to reinforce key concepts and measure progress.

By the end of this chapter, you'll have a meticulously planned course, complete with well-defined learning objectives and a structured content framework. Your course will not only educate but also inspire and empower your students, setting the stage for a transformative learning experience. With the groundwork laid, we'll move on to the exciting phase of creating your course content in Chapter 4. Get ready to bring your lessons to life and make a lasting impact!

Chapter 4

Creating Engaging Course Content

Choosing the Right Content Format (Video, Text, Audio, etc.)

Congratulations on reaching the creative heart of your online course creation journey! In this chapter, we'll explore the art of crafting compelling and engaging course content that captivates your audience and enhances their learning experience. From choosing the right content format to integrating interactive and multimedia elements, you'll learn how to transform your expertise into a dynamic and immersive educational adventure.

1. Choosing the Right Content Format

Video Lessons: Video content provides a personal touch, allowing students to connect with you as the instructor. Create well-scripted and visually appealing video lessons that break down complex topics. Visual demonstrations, animations, and real-life examples can make your lessons more engaging and memorable.

Text-Based Materials: Text-based content, such as articles, PDFs, and eBooks, offers a structured and in-depth exploration of your course topics. Use clear and concise language, break down information into digestible sections, and include visuals like images and infographics to enhance comprehension.

Audio Lessons and Podcasts: Audio content is perfect for learners on the go. Create podcasts or audio lessons that students can listen to during their commute, workout, or downtime. Ensure clear and articulate narration, and consider inviting guest speakers or experts to add variety and depth to your audio content.

Interactive Webinars: Host live interactive webinars or Q&A sessions where students can ask questions in real time. Webinars foster a sense of community among learners and provide opportunities for direct engagement with the course material and fellow participants.

Developing Interactive and Multimedia Elements

Quizzes and Assessments: Integrate quizzes and assessments throughout your course to reinforce learning and measure progress. Include a mix of multiple-choice questions, short answers, and practical exercises. Immediate feedback on quiz performance enhances the learning experience and helps students gauge their understanding.

Discussion Forums: Create discussion forums or online communities where students can share ideas, ask questions, and collaborate with peers. Active participation in discussions fosters a sense of community, encourages critical thinking, and provides diverse perspectives on course topics.

Interactive Assignments: Design hands-on assignments that encourage students to apply their knowledge and skills. Projects, case studies, group activities, and peer reviews enhance active learning, making the course content more tangible and relevant.

Visual Aids and Infographics: Visual elements such as charts, graphs, and infographics can simplify complex concepts and enhance understanding. Use visually appealing slides, diagrams, and illustrations in your video lessons and presentations to complement your explanations.

Guest Speakers and Interviews: Invite guest speakers or industry experts for interviews or collaborative sessions. Guest appearances add credibility to your course and offer diverse viewpoints. These interactions can provide valuable insights and inspire students by showcasing real-world applications of the course content.

By incorporating a variety of content formats and interactive elements, you'll create a rich and engaging learning experience for your students. Remember, the key is to align the content format with the course objectives and the preferences of your target audience. With a well-rounded approach to course content, you'll not only educate but also inspire and empower your students, making your online course an invaluable and transformative learning resource.

Chapter 5

Choosing the Right Platform

Comparing Different E-Learning Platforms

Congratulations on reaching a crucial crossroads in your online course creation journey! In this chapter, we'll navigate the labyrinth of e-learning platforms, helping you understand the diverse options available and empowering you to make an informed decision.

1. Comparing Different E-Learning Platforms

Diverse Platform Features: Explore the features offered by various e-learning platforms. Some platforms focus on video-based courses, while others offer interactive quizzes, discussion forums, and certification options. Evaluate these features based on your course requirements and desired student engagement level.

User-Friendliness: Consider the platform's user interface and ease of use. An intuitive platform simplifies the course creation process, making it effortless for you to upload content, manage students, and monitor course analytics. A user-friendly experience enhances both your workflow and your students' learning journey.

Customization Options: Assess the platform's customization capabilities. Can you brand your course and create a personalized learning environment? Customization allows you to showcase your unique identity, reinforcing your course's credibility and professionalism.

Pricing Structure: Compare the pricing models of different platforms. Some platforms charge a flat fee, while others operate on a revenue-sharing basis. Factor in your budget and revenue goals when evaluating pricing options. Additionally, consider any hidden costs and transaction fees associated with the platform.

Support and Resources: Investigate the level of customer support and available resources provided by each platform. A responsive support team can be invaluable, especially if you encounter technical issues or need assistance with course setup. Platforms that offer a comprehensive knowledge base, tutorials, and community forums empower you to troubleshoot independently.

Selecting the Best Platform for Your Needs

Define Your Requirements: Clearly outline your course requirements, including content formats, interactivity features, and desired learning outcomes. Knowing your needs will help you narrow down the options and focus on platforms that align with your vision.

Read Reviews and Testimonials: Research user reviews and testimonials from instructors who have used the platforms you're considering. Real-life experiences and feedback provide valuable insights into the platform's strengths, limitations, and overall user satisfaction.

Explore Trial Periods: Whenever possible, take advantage of free trial periods offered by e-learning platforms. During this time, explore the platform's features, upload sample content, and simulate the student experience. Hands-on exploration will help you assess the platform's suitability for your course.

Consider Future Scalability: Think long-term. Choose a platform that not only meets your current needs but also accommodates your future growth. Scalability is vital, especially if you plan to expand your course offerings or incorporate advanced features as your online teaching venture evolves.

Community and Networking: Some platforms foster a sense of community among instructors and learners. Evaluate the platform's community features, such as discussion forums and networking opportunities. Engaging with a supportive community can enhance your teaching experience and provide valuable networking opportunities.

By carefully comparing different e-learning platforms and selecting the one that aligns with your course requirements, budget, and long-term goals, you'll establish a solid foundation for your online course business. With the platform in place, you're now poised to transform your course vision into a reality.

Chapter 6

Designing a User-Friendly Course Interface

Creating an Intuitive Navigation System

Welcome to the digital storefront of your online course! In this chapter, we'll explore the art of designing a user-friendly course interface that captivates your audience from the moment they log in. By creating an intuitive navigation system and customizing the look and feel of your course, you'll provide your students with a seamless and engaging learning experience, ensuring they stay focused, motivated, and eager to absorb your valuable knowledge.

1. Creating an Intuitive Navigation System

Logical Course Structure: Organize your course content logically and sequentially. Divide the content into modules, units, or lessons, ensuring a clear progression. Students should easily understand where they are in the course and what topics they'll cover next.

A well-structured course minimizes confusion and enhances the learning journey.

User-Friendly Menus: Implement user-friendly menus and navigation buttons. Use clear and descriptive labels for course sections and modules. Avoid jargon and technical terms, opting for language that resonates with your target audience. Intuitive menus empower students to navigate effortlessly, accessing the content they need without frustration.

Interactive Syllabus: Provide an interactive syllabus or roadmap that outlines the course's objectives, schedule, and assignments. Include clickable links to each module or lesson, allowing students to jump directly to specific topics. An interactive syllabus enhances accessibility and encourages exploration.

Search Functionality: If applicable, incorporate a search function within your course platform. A search bar enables students to quickly locate specific topics or keywords, saving time and ensuring they find relevant information efficiently.

Customizing the Look and Feel of Your Course

Branding Consistency: Maintain consistent branding elements throughout your course. Use your logo, color scheme, and font choices to reinforce your brand identity. Consistency instills trust and professionalism, reinforcing your course's credibility.

Engaging Visuals: Incorporate engaging visuals, such as high-quality images, graphics, and videos. Visual elements break up the text, making the content more visually appealing and digestible. Use visuals to emphasize key points, create interest, and enhance the overall learning experience.

Readability and Accessibility: Prioritize readability by choosing clear and legible fonts. Use adequate spacing, headings, and bullet points to improve text comprehension. Additionally, ensure your course is accessible to all learners, including those with disabilities. Provide alternative text for images and ensure video content includes captions and transcripts.

Mobile Responsiveness: Design your course interface to be mobile-responsive. Many students access courses on smartphones and tablets. A mobile-friendly interface ensures a seamless experience across various devices, accommodating learners' preferences and lifestyles.

Engagement Features: Integrate interactive elements such as quizzes, polls, and discussion forums directly within the course interface. Interactive features foster engagement, encouraging students to participate actively. Well-placed calls-to-action prompt students to interact with the content, increasing their involvement and motivation.

By focusing on an intuitive navigation system and customizing the look and feel of your course, you create a user-friendly environment where students can immerse themselves in the learning process. A well-designed interface enhances engagement, fosters a sense of belonging, and ultimately contributes to your students' success. With your course interface expertly crafted, you're now prepared to move forward to Chapter 7, where we'll delve into the realm of optimizing your course for search engines (SEO) to attract more students. Get ready to make your course shine brightly in the digital landscape!

Chapter 7

Optimizing for Search Engines (SEO)

Understanding SEO Basics for Online Courses

Welcome to the digital marketing frontier of your online course venture! In this chapter, we'll demystify the art and science of Search Engine Optimization (SEO) specifically tailored for online courses. By understanding SEO basics and implementing strategic techniques, you'll amplify your course's visibility, attract more students, and establish a robust online presence that sets you apart in the competitive e-learning landscape.

Keyword Research: Start by identifying relevant keywords related to your course topic. Utilize keyword research tools to discover popular search terms that potential students might use. Long-tail keywords, which are more specific phrases, often yield better results as they target a niche audience interested in precise topics.

On-Page SEO: Optimize your course website or landing page with on-page SEO techniques. This includes optimizing meta titles, meta descriptions, and headers with relevant keywords. Ensure your content is well-structured, easy to read, and mobile-friendly. Search engines prioritize user experience, so a well-designed and accessible website is crucial.

Quality Content: Content is king in the world of SEO. Create high-quality, valuable, and informative content that addresses your audience's needs. Regularly update your course content and provide fresh, engaging materials. Engaging content not only attracts students but also encourages them to share your course with others, boosting your online presence.

Implementing SEO Strategies to Attract More Students

Backlink Building: Earn high-quality backlinks from reputable websites within your niche. Backlinks act as endorsements for your course's credibility. Collaborate with influencers, guest post on relevant blogs, or participate in industry forums. Quality backlinks improve your search engine rankings and drive organic traffic to your course.

Social Media Engagement: Leverage social media platforms to promote your course and engage with potential students. Share informative content, host live sessions, and actively participate in relevant discussions. Social signals, such as likes, shares, and comments, contribute to your online visibility. Encourage satisfied students to leave positive reviews and testimonials, enhancing your course's reputation.

Local SEO (if applicable): If your course caters to a specific location or demographic, optimize for local SEO. Create a Google My Business profile and ensure your course information, including address, phone number, and website, is accurate. Local directories and citations further boost your local search presence.

User Experience Optimization: Prioritize user experience on your course platform. A seamless, intuitive, and fast-loading website enhances user satisfaction and reduces bounce rates. Search engines reward websites that provide excellent user experiences with higher rankings.

Mobile Optimization: With the increasing prevalence of mobile device usage, ensure your course website is optimized for mobile platforms. Google prioritizes mobile-friendly websites in its search rankings. Responsive design and mobile-friendly interfaces enhance user experience and contribute to better SEO rankings.

By mastering the art of SEO, you'll position your online course for success in the digital realm. Implementing these strategies not only boosts your course's visibility but also attracts a steady stream of eager learners. With your course optimized to its full potential.

Chapter 8

Setting the Right Price

Pricing Strategies for Online Courses

Welcome to the chapter where strategy meets value, and your course transforms from knowledge into a valuable commodity. In this chapter, we'll delve into the intricate art of setting the right price for your online course. By understanding various pricing strategies and determining the true value of your course, you'll strike the perfect balance between affordability for your students and sustainability for your thriving online course business.

1. Pricing Strategies for Online Courses

Value-Based Pricing: Determine the value your course provides to your students. Consider the knowledge, skills, and transformational impact they'll gain. Price your course based on this perceived value. If your course offers unique insights, expert guidance, or exclusive resources, you can justify a premium price.

Competitive Pricing: Research similar courses within your niche to understand the price range. While you should not undervalue your course, aligning your price with the market average ensures that potential students perceive your course as competitively priced. Highlight unique features or bonuses to differentiate your offering.

Tiered Pricing: Offer different pricing tiers with varying levels of access or additional resources. For example, you can have a basic tier with core content, a standard tier with additional materials, and a premium tier with exclusive one-on-one coaching or advanced modules. Tiered pricing caters to a wider audience and provides options for different budgets.

Subscription Models: Consider offering subscription-based access, where students pay a recurring fee for ongoing access to your course content and updates. Subscriptions create a steady revenue stream and encourage long-term engagement. Ensure your course provides continuous value to justify the recurring payments.

Determining the Value of Your Course

Unique Selling Proposition (USP): Identify your course's unique selling points that set it apart from competitors. Whether it's your teaching approach, specialized knowledge, or comprehensive resources, clearly define what makes your course exceptional. Emphasize these points when communicating the value to potential students.

Transformative Potential: Assess the transformative potential of your course. How will it impact students' lives or careers? Will it help them gain valuable skills, advance in their professions, or achieve personal growth? A course that leads to tangible outcomes and positive transformations holds significant value for students.

Student Testimonials: Gather testimonials from previous students who have benefited from your course. Real-life success stories and positive feedback provide social proof of your course's value. Testimonials create trust and credibility, influencing potential students' perceptions of your course's worth.

Continuous Support: If your course includes ongoing support, mentoring, or community engagement, highlight this value. Access to expert guidance, peer networking, or exclusive forums enhances the learning experience. The assurance of continuous support adds value and justifies the course price.

Up-to-date Content: Regularly update your course content to keep it relevant and valuable. In rapidly evolving fields, up-to-date information is essential. Highlight your commitment to providing current, accurate, and valuable content, assuring students that they're investing in knowledge that remains pertinent over time.

By understanding the intricacies of pricing strategies and accurately determining the value of your course, you'll establish a pricing model that attracts students, sustains your business, and reflects the true worth of your educational offering.

Chapter 9

Effective Course Launch Strategies

Building Anticipation before Launch

Welcome to the chapter where your course takes its grand stage, and your hard work transforms into a tangible, thriving educational venture. In this chapter, we'll explore the art of executing a successful course launch. By building anticipation before the launch and implementing strategic tactics, you'll create buzz, captivate your audience, and ensure that your course gains the attention it deserves.

1. Building Anticipation Before Launch

Create Teasers and Sneak Peeks: Generate excitement by offering teasers and sneak peeks of your course content. Share intriguing snippets, behind-the-scenes footage, or snippets of student testimonials. These teasers provide a glimpse into the value your course offers, piquing curiosity and anticipation among potential students.

Engage in Content Marketing: Leverage content marketing strategies to build anticipation. Create blog posts, videos, podcasts, or infographics related to your course topic. Share valuable insights, tips, or case studies to establish your expertise and attract an audience interested in your niche. Content marketing not only drives organic traffic but also positions you as an authority in your field.

Harness the Power of Social Media: Utilize social media platforms to create anticipation. Share visually appealing graphics, engaging polls, or interactive quizzes related to your course topic. Encourage your audience to share their expectations or goals, creating a sense of community excitement. Social media platforms provide a dynamic space for building hype and connecting with potential students.

Email Marketing Campaigns: Build an email list of interested individuals and nurture their interest through targeted email marketing campaigns. Send informative newsletters, countdown emails, or exclusive pre-launch offers to your subscribers. Personalize your messages and emphasize the unique benefits of your course. Email marketing allows for direct communication and relationship building, fostering a loyal audience base.

Launching Your Course Successfully

Offer Early-Bird Discounts or Bonuses: Create a sense of urgency by offering early-bird discounts or exclusive bonuses to students who enroll during the launch period. Limited-time offers encourage swift action, driving initial enrollments. Highlight the value of these offers and emphasize the benefits of early enrollment, such as access to exclusive content or personalized coaching sessions.

Host a Launch Webinar or Live Event: Host a live launch event, such as a webinar or Facebook Live session, where you introduce your course, share success stories, and interact with your audience in real time. Engage with attendees, answer questions, and provide additional insights into your course content. Live events create a buzz, enhance credibility, and offer a unique opportunity to connect with potential students directly.

Leverage Influencer Partnerships: Collaborate with influencers or experts in your field to promote your course. Influencers can reach a broader audience and lend credibility to your offering. Offer them complimentary access to your course and request their honest feedback or testimonials. Their endorsement can significantly impact potential students' trust and interest in your course.

Encourage Word-of-mouth Marketing: Encourage satisfied students to share their experiences and recommendations with their networks. Offer referral bonuses or discounts for students who refer others to your course. Positive word-of-mouth marketing is incredibly powerful and can exponentially expand your course's reach.

Collect and Showcase Testimonials: Gather testimonials from early enrollees or beta testers who have experienced your course. Positive testimonials provide social proof of your course's value and authenticity. Display these testimonials prominently on your course website, marketing materials, and social media platforms. Genuine praise from satisfied students instills confidence in potential enrollees.

By effectively building anticipation before launch and executing a well-planned launch strategy, you'll generate buzz, attract eager learners, and set the stage for a successful course journey.

Chapter 10

Marketing Your Course

Utilizing Social Media and Email Marketing

Congratulations on launching your course! Now, it's time to ensure that your valuable content reaches the widest audience possible. In this chapter, we'll explore the essential strategies for marketing your course effectively. By harnessing the power of social media and email marketing, as well as leveraging collaborations and partnerships, you'll expand your reach, engage potential students, and build a thriving community around your course.

1. Utilizing Social Media and Email Marketing

Strategic Social Media Presence: Utilize social media platforms strategically. Identify the platforms where your target audience is most active and focus your efforts there. Share engaging content related to your course, such as informative articles, video snippets, student testimonials, and interactive polls. Foster a sense of community by responding to comments, encouraging discussions, and addressing queries promptly.

Email Marketing Campaigns: Continue to leverage email marketing to nurture your relationship with existing and potential students. Send regular newsletters with valuable content, updates, and exclusive offers. Segment your email list based on student's interests or engagement levels to send targeted and personalized messages. Use compelling subject lines and visually appealing email templates to increase open rates.

Automated Drip Campaigns: Implement automated drip campaigns to deliver a series of pre-scheduled emails to new subscribers or leads. Drip campaigns can introduce your course, share success stories, offer free resources, and gradually nurture leads into enrollments. Tailor the content and timing of the emails based on the recipient's interactions and interests, maximizing the chances of conversion.

Collaborations and Partnerships for Course Promotion

Influencer Collaborations: Partner with influencers, bloggers, or YouTubers in your niche to promote your course. Influencers can create authentic content, such as reviews, tutorials, or interviews, reaching their established audience with your course offerings. Collaborations with influencers provide credibility and access to a broader, targeted audience.

Affiliate Marketing: Implement an affiliate marketing program where individuals or businesses promote your course in exchange for a commission on successful enrollments. Affiliates can include bloggers, industry experts, or even satisfied students who want to recommend your course. Provide affiliates with promotional materials, tracking tools, and attractive commissions to incentivize their efforts.

Strategic Partnerships: Form strategic partnerships with organizations, institutions, or businesses related to your course topic. Collaborate on joint events, workshops, or webinars. Partnerships can provide cross-promotion opportunities, expanding your reach to a relevant and interested audience. Highlight the mutual benefits of the partnership to attract partners who align with your course's objectives.

Guest Blogging and Podcast Appearances: Contribute guest posts to popular blogs in your niche or participate as a guest on relevant podcasts. Sharing your expertise with a new audience establishes your authority and can drive traffic to your course website. Include links to your course or offer exclusive discounts to the audience of the blog or podcast you're collaborating with.

By effectively utilizing social media and email marketing, as well as forming strategic collaborations and partnerships, you'll create a powerful marketing engine for your online course. Continuously monitor your marketing efforts, track key metrics, and adjust your strategies based on the results. With a well-executed marketing plan, you'll attract enthusiastic learners, nurture a vibrant community, and position your course as a leading authority in your field.

Chapter 11

Providing Excellent Student Support

Handling Student Inquiries and Feedback

Welcome to the chapter where student satisfaction takes center stage! In this chapter, we'll explore the vital aspects of providing exceptional support to your students. By effectively handling inquiries and feedback and creating a supportive learning community, you'll foster a positive educational experience, ensuring your students feel valued, engaged, and empowered throughout their learning journey.

1. Handling Student Inquiries and Feedback

Timely and Personalized Responses: Respond promptly to student inquiries and feedback. Personalize your responses, addressing students by name and demonstrating genuine interest in their concerns. Timely and personalized communication reassures students that their questions are valued and encourages active engagement.

FAQs and Knowledge Base: Anticipate common questions by creating a comprehensive Frequently Asked Questions (FAQs) section or knowledge base. Organize information logically, covering topics such as course navigation, technical support, and content-related queries. A well-structured resource can empower students to find answers independently, enhancing their learning experience.

Interactive Q&A Sessions: Host regular live Q&A sessions where students can ask questions in real-time. Use platforms like webinars, live chats, or discussion forums to facilitate interactive sessions. Q&A sessions provide immediate clarifications, address uncertainties, and create a sense of community among learners.

Feedback Loops: Encourage students to provide feedback on various aspects of the course, such as content relevance, instructional methods, and overall experience. Create surveys, polls, or feedback forms to gather structured input. Analyze feedback systematically and implement improvements based on students' suggestions. Acknowledge feedback openly, demonstrating your commitment to enhancing the course.

Creating a Supportive Learning Community

Discussion Forums and Community Spaces: Establish discussion forums or online community spaces where students can connect, collaborate, and share insights. Actively participate in discussions, address queries, and encourage positive interactions. A vibrant learning community fosters a sense of belonging, encourages knowledge exchange, and enhances engagement.

Peer Interaction Opportunities: Design group activities, peer reviews, or collaborative projects that encourage students to interact and learn from one another. Peer interactions promote diverse perspectives, stimulate critical thinking, and create a supportive network. Facilitate structured opportunities for students to collaborate, fostering a collaborative and inclusive learning environment.

Supportive Feedback Culture: Cultivate a supportive feedback culture within the community. Encourage constructive criticism and respectful discussions. Provide guidelines for giving and receiving feedback to maintain a positive atmosphere. Acknowledge and appreciate students who contribute valuable insights, reinforcing a culture of mutual respect and continuous improvement.

Moderation and Guidance: Moderate discussions to ensure a respectful and inclusive environment. Intervene if necessary to address inappropriate behavior or conflicts. Provide clear guidelines for respectful communication and intervene promptly if any issues arise. A well-moderated community ensures a safe space for students to express themselves and engage with the course content and peers.

By focusing on excellent student support, you'll create a nurturing learning environment where students feel supported, motivated, and inspired. A responsive and engaged instructor, combined with a supportive community, contributes significantly to student satisfaction and success.

Chapter 12

Analyzing Course Performance

Monitoring Student Engagement and Progress

Welcome to the chapter where data-driven insights guide the evolution of your online course! In this chapter, we'll explore the crucial aspects of analyzing course performance. By monitoring student engagement and progress and leveraging analytics, you'll gain valuable insights into your course's effectiveness. Armed with this knowledge, you can continuously refine your teaching methods, content, and overall course experience, ensuring your students receive the best possible education.

1. Monitoring Student Engagement and Progress

Tracking Student Activity: Utilize learning management system (LMS) analytics to monitor student activity. Track metrics such as login frequency, time spent on lessons, quiz participation, and content downloads. Identify patterns in student behavior to understand which sections of your course are most engaging and where students might be facing challenges.

Assessing Quiz and Assignment Performance: Analyze quiz and assignment results to gauge student comprehension. Identify questions with low success rates to pinpoint challenging topics. Use this data to revise or provide additional resources for challenging concepts. Celebrate student achievements and progress, fostering motivation and confidence.

Participation in Interactive Elements: Evaluate student participation in interactive elements like discussion forums, live Q&A sessions, and collaborative projects. Active participation indicates a vibrant learning community. Monitor engagement levels and intervene if participation drops, encouraging student interaction and collaboration.

Using Analytics to Improve Your Course

Identifying Dropout Points: Analyze the data to identify dropout points in your course. Dropout points are stages where students tend to disengage or withdraw. Investigate these points to understand the challenges students face. Revise content, offer additional support, or enhance explanations to address common dropout triggers.

Assessing Learning Objectives: Evaluate students' performance concerning the course learning objectives. Determine if students are mastering the intended skills and knowledge. If specific objectives consistently show low attainment rates, consider revising your teaching methods, providing additional resources, or offering targeted support to help students achieve these goals.

Analyzing Feedback and Surveys: Analyze feedback gathered from surveys and student reviews. Look for recurring themes or suggestions for improvement. Address the issues raised by students and implement changes based on their feedback. Regularly surveying students provides ongoing insights, allowing you to adapt your course in response to evolving needs and preferences.

A/B Testing and Experimentation: Implement A/B testing by offering variations of certain course elements to different groups of students. Compare the performance and engagement levels between these groups to determine what works best. Experiment with different teaching styles, content formats, or interactive elements to identify the most effective approaches.

Continuous Iteration: Use the insights gained from analytics to iterate and enhance your course continuously. Regularly update content, improve explanations, and integrate new resources based on student behavior and feedback. Embrace a mindset of continuous improvement, adapting your course to cater to the dynamic learning needs of your students.

By harnessing the power of analytics, you'll transform raw data into actionable insights, driving the ongoing refinement of your online course. Regular analysis and adaptation based on student engagement and performance metrics are key to ensuring your course remains relevant, engaging, and impactful. As you delve into the world of course performance analysis, you're now prepared to embark on the journey of educational excellence, shaping the future of your online course and the educational experiences of your students.

Chapter 13

Scaling Your Online Course Business

Expanding Your Course Offerings

Welcome to the chapter where your online course business transforms from a single offering into a thriving educational empire! In this chapter, we'll explore the strategies for scaling your online course business. By expanding your course offerings and implementing automation, you'll unlock the potential for exponential growth, reaching a broader audience and maximizing the impact of your expertise.

1. Expanding Your Course Offerings

Diversifying Course Topics: Identify related or complementary topics within your expertise and create additional courses. Diversifying your offerings caters to a broader audience with varied interests. Consider creating beginner, intermediate, and advanced levels of your courses to accommodate learners at different skill levels.

Specialized Workshops and Masterclasses: Offer specialized workshops, masterclasses, or boot camps that delve deep into specific topics. These intensive, focused sessions cater to students seeking in-depth knowledge or hands-on experiences. Limited-time or exclusive workshops create a sense of urgency, driving enrollments.

SubscriptionBased Models: Introduce subscription-based models where students pay a monthly or yearly fee for access to a library of courses. Subscription models provide recurring revenue and incentivize students to explore multiple courses within your platform. Regularly update your course offerings to maintain subscriber engagement.

Automating Processes for Scalability

Automated Enrollment and Onboarding: Implement automated enrollment and onboarding processes. Use email automation to send welcome emails, course access instructions, and introductory materials to new students. Streamlining the onboarding experience ensures a seamless start for every student, saving you time and effort.

Automated Assessments and Grading: Utilize learning management systems (LMS) that offer automated assessments and grading functionalities. Automated quizzes, assignments, and evaluations provide instant feedback to students, enhancing the learning experience. As an instructor, you can focus on interacting with students and providing personalized support.

Email Marketing Sequences: Develop email marketing sequences using marketing automation tools. Create automated email sequences for nurturing leads, promoting new courses, and engaging with existing students. Personalize the content based on students' interactions and preferences, nurturing relationships on autopilot.

Content Drip Campaigns: Implement content drip campaigns to deliver course materials progressively over time. Drip campaigns ensure a structured learning experience, preventing overwhelm for students while maintaining their engagement. Automate the release of modules, lessons, or bonus content, allowing students to pace their learning journey.

Customer Support Chatbots: Integrate chatbots on your website or course platform to handle frequently asked questions and provide instant responses. Chatbots can direct students to relevant resources, assist with technical issues, and offer basic course information. Human support can be reserved for more complex inquiries, optimizing your support team's efficiency.

By expanding your course offerings and embracing automation, you'll create a scalable online course business that can accommodate a growing student base. As you automate processes, you'll free up your time to focus on creating high-quality content, engaging with students, and strategizing further business expansion. With your scalable model in place, you're now equipped to explore the limitless possibilities of your online course empire, shaping the future of education and making a lasting impact on the lives of your students.

Conclusion

The Evolution of Online Learning

As we conclude this journey through the intricacies of online course creation, it's evident that the future of education is being transformed right before our eyes. The digital landscape has opened unprecedented opportunities for both educators and learners, enabling the creation of diverse, engaging, and accessible learning experiences. In this concluding chapter, let's reflect on the profound impact of online learning and explore the exciting trends and innovations that are shaping the e-learning industry's future.

Online learning has evolved from a novel concept into a powerful global phenomenon. With the advent of technology, learners no longer need to be confined to traditional classrooms; education has become borderless, and accessible to anyone, anywhere. The online courses created today empower individuals from all walks of life, fostering skill development, career advancement, and personal growth. The democratization of education is at the core of this digital revolution.

Trends and Innovations in the E-Learning Industry

Personalized Learning Paths: Adaptive learning technologies are tailoring educational experiences to individual students' needs, adjusting the pace and content based on their progress and proficiency. Personalized learning ensures that each student receives targeted support, maximizing their understanding and retention.

Immersive Learning Experiences: Virtual Reality (VR) and Augmented Reality (AR) are revolutionizing education by creating immersive, interactive learning environments. Students can explore historical sites, conduct virtual experiments, or engage in lifelike simulations, enhancing their understanding and engagement with the content.

Microlearning: Bite-sized learning modules, known as microlearning, are gaining popularity. These concise, focused lessons are designed for quick consumption, catering to learners' busy lifestyles. Microlearning modules are highly effective for just-in-time learning, allowing students to acquire specific skills or information efficiently.

Social Learning Communities: Collaborative learning platforms and social learning communities are fostering peer-to-peer interaction and knowledge sharing. Discussion forums, group projects, and interactive online communities create a sense of belonging, encouraging students to learn from one another and engage in meaningful discussions.

Blockchain and Credentialing: Blockchain technology is being explored for secure, transparent credential verification. Digital badges and certificates stored on blockchain provide immutable records of students' achievements, enhancing the credibility and portability of online credentials.

Embracing the Future

As educators, course creators, and lifelong learners, we stand at the threshold of a transformative era in education. Embracing these trends and innovations empowers us to craft rich, dynamic learning experiences that inspire, educate, and empower the next generation of thinkers, creators, and leaders.

In this ever-evolving landscape, the key lies in adaptability and a commitment to continuous improvement. By staying abreast of emerging technologies, understanding learners' evolving needs, and fostering a supportive, inclusive learning environment, we can shape the future of online learning and contribute to a world where education knows no boundaries.

As you embark on your educational ventures, remember that knowledge is a beacon guiding us toward a brighter, more connected future. By harnessing the power of online learning and embracing the innovative spirit that defines this era, we can truly transform lives and pave the way for a global community of lifelong learners. Here's to the future of education, an inspiring journey where the pursuit of knowledge knows no limits.

www.ingramcontent.com/pod-product-compliance
Lightning Source LLC
Chambersburg PA
CBHW062250290526
45794CB00006B/2489

* 9   7   9   8   8   6   6   7   2   2   2   8   0 *